T0129854

50 Possibilities for Increasing Your Personal-Power™

Dr. Marie Roberts De La Parra

BALBOA.PRESS

A DIVISION OF HAY HOUSE

Copyright © 2022 Dr. Marie Roberts De La Parra.

All rights reserved. No part of this book may be used or reproduced by any means, graphic, electronic, or mechanical, including photocopying, recording, taping or by any information storage retrieval system without the written permission of the author except in the case of brief quotations embodied in critical articles and reviews.

Balboa Press books may be ordered through booksellers or by contacting:

Balboa Press
A Division of Hay House
1663 Liberty Drive
Bloomington, IN 47403
www.balboapress.com
844-682-1282

Because of the dynamic nature of the Internet, any web addresses or links contained in this book may have changed since publication and may no longer be valid. The views expressed in this work are solely those of the author and do not necessarily reflect the views of the publisher, and the publisher hereby disclaims any responsibility for them.

The author of this book does not dispense medical advice or prescribe the use of any technique as a form of treatment for physical, emotional, or medical problems without the advice of a physician, either directly or indirectly. The intent of the author is only to offer information of a general nature to help you in your quest for emotional and spiritual well-being. In the event you use any of the information in this book for yourself, which is your constitutional right, the author and the publisher assume no responsibility for your actions.

Any people depicted in stock imagery provided by Getty Images are models, and such images are being used for illustrative purposes only. Certain stock imagery © Getty Images.

Print information available on the last page.

ISBN: 979-8-7652-3315-3 (sc)
ISBN: 979-8-7652-3313-9 (hc)
ISBN: 979-8-7652-3314-6 (e)

Library of Congress Control Number: 2022915305

Balboa Press rev. date: 08/23/2022

To B, who showed me how to grow up

Contents

By Marie Roberts De La Parra

Introduction

Self-worth is not net-worth. This quote is from one of my social media posts from the aftermath of the 2008 economic and housing crisis, a vital learning experience for my future financial, mental, and emotional empowerment. As a single parent, I had no idea how I would take care of my child or myself. We no longer had a home; my resources were all gone. What do you do when you just can't think about going through another day of depression, stress, anguish, and having the feeling of being alone in the experience? Shame can kill you if you let it!

At the time and for a long while, all I saw before me was my failure. I had to teach myself that my worth was never connected to anything material; my worth came from within. My worth came from my state of being, and from my strategizing "to win in my thinking, to win everywhere." I began teaching myself how to be victorious in thought to alter my mental, emotional, and external condition through the development of possibilities. This was a journey that changed my mindset and self-belief, and where I gained important and principle self-awareness and self-knowledge.

A key finding was locating my modus operandi, where I sought to address the many wrongs I had caused so that they would be "righted." I also wanted to understand the pain I felt was inflicted upon me. I wanted to have an unfathomable understanding and insight into the goings on of my life as well as the happenings of others. As I worked on these practices for myself, I discovered that glancing in the mirror and admitting that somewhere, somehow you have willingly and wildly gone astray, is not an easy task. However, it is a pathway that reveals the requirements of how to grow to become the foremost version of you, which is always ongoing.

My journey has allowed me to now see my life, my reflection, in the lives of the many very clearly. I recognized my journey was not only for or about me. I hope that my findings will be an asset to you.

This book contains 50 possibilities of perceptions and some unknown blind spots I discovered in my pathway that gave me insight into my happenings as well as those of others. The vitality—the light within each of us that makes us beam with enthusiastic positivity, energizing our life—is what I refer to as Personal-Power™. Your Personal-Power™ is the personal mixology that makes you, you. We each show up in different ways.

Now, my lifestyle implementation is to be the most dynamic me that I created and desired to be, greeting each day with enthusiasm for having another day living a life that I love, appreciate, and am passionate about. It takes regular practice, work, and effort. My wish, my prayer, and my purpose are to support all of life in experiencing and feeling the joy in living a life of love.

I appreciate you,
Marie

Author's Note

This book consists of 50 possibilities for understanding, developing, and increasing your Personal-Power™. Each power is essential to me. I found that the easiest way to incorporate these possibilities into your life is to develop a practice of working on one for an entire week as a way to obtain self-awareness and self-knowledge about how you are being.

I recommend the following best practice strategy. First, read through the whole book. As you review the 50 possibilities, pay attention and highlight the information that most resonates and aligns with and for you. As you move through the list of the powers, start making a list of the powers you would like to develop and/or understand, placing them in a specified sequence to indicate the powers that are most important to you. Then, go back to the top of your list and start with reading only one power for one week in the morning of each day. During the day, spend some time thinking on the power and the self-information you gain from it, making notes about how you use the power during your day. Learn about yourself by deciding to actively engage with your power and identifying how effectively you can make use and magnify the power to generate and increase your enthusiasm and life energy. Consider ways that you can personalize what you do with each power and share it with and for others.

Choose each day to be more gracious, considerate, and compassionate with the use of your power. Be mindful of how you show up for yourself, as well as how you show up for others.

I believe that by committing yourself to using the methods shared here, they will help you in self-mastery and release the presence of energy unique to you, empowering you to "Be" the most authentic transparent version of you. These methods will help you to do you, well.

Self-Knowledge increases and magnifies your Personal-Power™, and every time you dispense energy on negative thoughts, negative words, and/or mood swings, you give your power all away, diminishing your life essence, your light, and your self-control.

Power-1
Personal-Power™

Almost all of us experience life challenges; amid my most difficult ones, I started to see that I was willingly giving away what was notable to having a favorable fulfilling life: my Personal-Power™. In those moments, I recognized that, when we are each filled with a positive mindset, we feel lighthearted, worthy, have more sensations of joy, and radiate what gives us our essence, drawing those same qualities in others to us. Personal-Power™ is something that everyone is born with, and we either learn to grow and develop the power, or we learn how to let ourselves and others extinguish what energizes, illuminates, and connects us to the core of our state of being.

Your Personal-Power™ exists to fill you up, and your ability to live a harmonious, commanding life flourish when you continuously give to the power that already exists within you. When you have obtained the capability to replenish your Personal-Power™ with ease, it will never leave you. By doing so, you will then have the skillfulness to share it effectively to nourish others.

Those thoughts you think can never be kept secret.

Power-2
Intention-Power

The things we want and seek to create our desires can appear in moments that represent both the good and the bad in our experiences, our lessons. Your thoughts, words, and actions determine the love, compassion, and care present in the positive outcome of a thing, a being, a person. So, you must identify what you would like to aim your Intention Power toward. Having no idea of how I was being in my former state left me without the understanding of how my line of thinking was bound like a constrictor knot to the love I sought, which was my own. I focused only on getting what I thought that I wanted, and what I felt I desperately needed, all the while paying no attention to the required and vital details, which might contain a hidden purpose.

When I discovered that I could not get nor give away something I didn't already give to myself first, I became a transformational leader regarding all my actions, invigorating my life. Hence, I learned that manifesting with self-love allows for the positive things you desire and seek in life to arrive because love is <u>not</u> based on what someone else does; love is dependent only on what you do, especially in your thinking.

Appreciate yourself before you go expecting someone else to do it for you.

Power-3
Self-Recognition-Power

"I gave you a gift, but you don't even appreciate it." These 11 words say so much about the real aim, to be appreciated, which is the very opposite of giving. You or somebody you know spouts these same words. So, before you go on a bend to seek validation from another, the acknowledgement you seek should be coming from you. Be invaluable to you. Show how much you care by honoring who you are through your realization of self-appreciation. Hold yourself accountable for how you want to feel by the use of your Self-Recognition-Power.

Doing kind things does not make you a kind person.

Power-4
Altruistic-Power

Have you been kind to someone because you like who they are and what they do one day, but they don't act, or appear the same the next day, so you take all your kindness away? Authentic compassion does not require you to try to be kind; it demands it of you. Picking and choosing when to be kind and who to be kind to will disempower you and cause yourself and others to be confused as to who you really are. The goal is to have Altruistic-Power in each action you take. To embody Altruistic-Power, practice thinking and giving warmheartedness throughout all of your life and toward everyone you greet, no matter what goes on. The paramount time to be kind is when someone rubs you the wrong way; this will be an advantageous task and your teachable moment. To be in receipt of kindness almost everywhere you go, use your Altruistic-Power by giving your kindness first before someone has to think about it. By engaging in this practice, some kindliness will undoubtedly show up when you need it the most.

*Get to know and be comfortable
with all of you.*

Power-5
Doing-You-Power

If you don't have an interest in knowing who you are, why would you expect anyone else to make such an effort? No one should understand you better than you do. Never make your new car manual more important than getting to know who you are. Spend time in your life to create your very own uniqueness manual that contains your personal directive. The effort you took to get the highest score to pass your very first driver's license exam, thus expanding your freedom, is the same diligence you must take in fostering your Doing-You-Power.

*Presenting good thoughts to your
psyche will make you unstoppable
in your mission and your tasks.*

Power-6
Perception-Power

The Perception-Power will assist you in having well-directed thoughts. Using this power, you will highlight the solace in everything you wish to do and set out to design. Regardless of your task, whether it be big or small, daunting or repetitious, what you think about it will be your strategic key. Find the lenses of joy in whatever the duty you have throughout your charge, as you create the delight inside everything you accomplish; it is always about how you look upon it.

You are never-failing; you are teaching yourself how you win.

Power-7
Vanquishing-Power

So, today, you were told you didn't qualify; maybe you didn't get the new contract or the job at the new business you knew was a perfect fit. Whatever it is you perceive to be a loss, never give up or give in to the challenge. Your tenacity will be what allows you to discover your win. Go to sleep for the night and remove the day's stress because tomorrow, you will have another chance to acquire the needed knowledge. You have spent the time to discover all the routes and paths, and what is left is your map of how to achieve what you desire: your secret diagram for removing all obstacles in your way. So, grasp and take hold of your Vanquishing-Power.

Declare and keep moving towards your central purpose; To do good.

Power-8
Virtue-Power

Generational-Good™ is something that is needed in each corner of the world at every moment. The size of your good is not a critical factor; to do good is the vital component. No matter the proportions of the good you implement, it has a positive ripple. If the good you can do is the size of a raindrop, then gather a thousand of those raindrops whenever they might fall and fill a barrel that will transform the thirst happening all over this planet. Don't let the moment of any day go by without you showcasing the good that is the essence of a high-quality state of being: your Virtue-Power.

*Know your intent in everything
you do because any hidden agenda
will be what you project; it will
be revealed sooner or later.*

Power-9
Source-Power

Know what you seek in your heart and go after it. It sounds like such an easy task, right? It is if you know you don't have a masked program, the type you don't even recognize within yourself until it happens. It can show up and throw you off track, appearing as envy, jealousy, resentfulness, and/or maliciousness, a common trap to get tangled in. This trap makes you weak and powerless, leading you to give all your energy to a negative cause.

Remember, to get what you say you deserve, make sure you know what your words mean and the actions you take to create them for either the good, the bad, or the beautiful. Prepare your self-efficacy for what your actual intent is. Then, work your hardest to accomplish your declared goal using your Source-Power.

Use your thoughts, words, actions, and focus to ensure you know what you are letting in; your life depends on it.

Power-10
Blissfulness-Power

Watch out; you might have a crevice opening in your pathway, letting what you don't want in. In powerful decision making, the key is to have your thoughts, words, and actions in alignment. Focus on what you are thinking and formulate the critical foundation for the long and arduous effort of centralizing your purposeful focal point. When your positive thoughts and affirmative words combine and align with your destined resolute actions, your Blissfulness-Power will feel like a magical agreement.

If you wish to see the truth of who you are, then release yourself of who you or anyone else thinks you need to be.

Power-11
Mirror-Power

Don't hold yourself hostage; free yourself because no one else can do it for you. Stop and use the key that unlocks the door from the comparison of who your past deeds still see yourself to be. Go now and look deep into your Mirror-Power as the overseer of you, with your ability to cast all that is remarkable from your inner looking glass. Once the decision is made to take over the ownership of your reflection, you will recognize the extraordinary beauty in what it means to be free to be magnificently you. The decision is always yours!

Always let love be your master and use love as the master over your money.

Power-12
Rapture-Power

Right now, too much of life is being lived transactionally, passing off material assets as love and well-being for ourselves and others. Stuff that is used to patch up the emotional cavities in us, making our money in control of our power. Yes, money is here to enhance comforts in life. However, without a watchful eye and self-understanding, spending can momentarily translate to feeling good and looking fabulous from the purchases until we meet up with that fleeting experience that requires us to fill up the need to get more of the same, developing a repetitious defeatist practice.

We so often forget that the ambiance and unalloyed emotion in and from love are sourced from compassion and empathy, giving off a high altitude of warmth and affection that's orchestrated as the Rapture-Power, which is harnessed when you yield assistance from your inner elements of strength. Master the use of this power over everything in your world.

The positive wishes you put upon somebody else will be there to meet you at your own door; the same is true of the reverse, the negative. So, make sure you understand and know that which you are really wishing for.

Power-13
Fulfillment-Power

Making a wish, a silent prayer, while hoping and believing it will come true often brings us such remarkable joy. When we hope for things for another, it is usually done with selflessness actions, never considering the boomerang effect that may be in store. The Fulfillment-Power comes into play whether the wish is for the splendor of someone or otherwise, and someday it will return to you, illuminated in the manner just as you wished it, regardless of when or whom you wished it for.

You can't choose how somebody responds to your apology; you can only choose to give it. Humble yourself and do it.

Power-14
Humility-Power

While in the process of forgiving, be sure to reflect and choose to forgive yourself for any of your missteps. The Humility-Power will fill you up with self-forgetfulness by offering up your hand of forgiveness and embracing an apology from another; it will supply you with a self-pardon when your request for forgiveness is not accepted, freeing you to chart on to a more serene, calm, and unstressed path, for you have done your best to address what you made wrong.

*First, learn to listen to yourself
if you want others to.*

Power-15
Alliance-Power

Most of us are waiting to be heard by others, and yet we pay so little attention to what our life has to say to and about us. We miss observing our lives, ignoring the repeated whisper when it says, "don't do that." We still choose to do it anyway. We keep driving on the road when every sign says, "turnaround, you're going the wrong way." We drive along until the warning sign is blinding red or until we have the collision where we can't just get up and walk away once again.

Pay attention; your life is calling you to be in partnership with it. Make use of your Alliance-Power. It is in your own best interest.

Rule your world. Wield your power wisely and effectively.

Power-16
Decree-Power

Learn to manage the self because time cannot be mastered. Time is not flexible, bendable, or movable; it will not be controlled. While attempting to manage time, the time keeps on moving. What are you able to master? You. Once you make use of the Decree-Power by establishing self-mastery, you will secure fluidity, flowing from moment to moment.

Guard your imagination so it won't get infected by those who fear to dream for having never learned to follow their own vision.

Power-17
Visionary-Power

You are filled with your thoughts, but not everyone makes use of their dreams. Your imagination requires you to get in step with the pathway that aligns you with your Visionary-Power. It is the center of your inventiveness, leading you to discover the things only you are here to puzzle out. Conceive of what only you are here to understand and generate your creativity.

*Freely give that which you seek
that is advantageous away once you
have developed it within yourself.*

Power-18
Benevolence-Power

When electing to donate money and resources to your selected charity, you must initially obtain the wherewithal that is required. It is near impossible to giveaway something not yet acquired because you don't want to get caught making promises that cannot be attained.

Once you've collected your bestowal, your gift, it is given without living in regret because your word and your promises to yourself are now being met. When giving your compassion and care, you must follow a similar practice in keeping in step with your actions, making yourself the initial test-case. Contribute to yourself the first dividend of your Benevolence-Power and then gift some daily to an individual's spiritual collection.

How much peace do your words bring for someone else's life because, in the stillness of your mind, you hold the key to every one of your causes?

Power-19
Tranquility-Power

Tranquility-Power is knowing when to hold your words and save them for another point in time or maybe hold onto them forever. It is not always beneficial to share what you are thinking, giving away your voice to all who will listen to your spontaneous and probably unsolicited advice. Just because you decide to say something, saying it does not make it so. What matters is the experience that your explaining gives; be sure to ask for permission before you dive in. The gift of gab should always be sprinkled first with supportiveness, making the encounter informative, illuminating, and reflective, which are the essential encouragements with communicating when you want someone to listen and lean in.

*Don't give yourself the daily beat down
you don't deserve because yesterday
you spent much of your energy
making all kinds of assumptions.*

Power-20
Valiant-Power

Calm yourself, slow down, and observe your life and how it is being lived. These are the moments when you have the opportunity to transform you and your relationships by taking a close look within. Watch, and you will see yourself projecting the experience you just had onto another. Much of the time, you are going off what you feel and not off what you have just learned because you have not yet acquired the desire to notice your personal occurrence. To detect accurately and view your evolvement without inventing a tale, your Valiant-Power must come into play; it takes audacity to pay attention to your life's happenings.

Get out of your way, then stay out.

Power-21
Door-Opening-Power

Been there done that, so why repeat that? How often in life does a repetitious situation happen, and goes on ignored? As we grow individually, life can become filled with purposeless noise. When essential details specifically for us show up, we discard them, placing them amongst all the other clamors. By paying limited if any attention to the movie we are starring in, we miss the path that raises and elevates our self-knowledge. So, I beacon you to rid yourself of the useless negative discord, a happening that does not have to be. Never forget you have the power to prevent these reoccurring events. Find your course of action to perceive what comes around to repeat itself, causing you to stand and block your good fortune. The Door-Opening-Power is active when one can remove the primary obstacle known as "you."

Remain positive in thought no matter who or what comes your way.

Power-22
Unbounded-Power

Your thoughts are shaping your character, your destiny, and how you address all circumstances that present on your path. You must be steadfast and hold your ground, never changing your positive positioning no matter who or what shows up to attack your spirit. Your ability to move beyond any perceived barrier is limitless; it is all based on how you discern and operate beyond it. Start with the removal of your mental roadblock, for then you will be efficacious with your remedy. Now, you have the overall effectiveness to design in thought, bringing anything to fruition: your Unbounded-Power.

*Know the high caliber you will receive
when you unconditionally give to
the self-worth of anyone else.*

Power-23
Meaningfulness-Power

All of life matters; there are no throwaways! Place all your efforts into accomplishing your mission, your goal, and your purpose to be a great contributor to someone else's dignity, self-respect, self-confidence, self-esteem, self-regard, and prestige. Building a people up, along with life, is a premier time for unveiling your Meaningfulness-Power.

When one is stifled and denied the ability to self-express, one is denied the ability to do and be their very best.

Power-24
Inventiveness-Power

Those ideas inside you are not only for the benefit of you. Make the most of them, for they lead you to your remarkable originality. Share with your world and the universe your distinctive imagination, your Inventiveness-Power. Your ideas shall make a world of difference. You will never know if you don't show up, step up, get out there, and do whatever it takes to bring about your designs. Let loose, freeing up your out-of-the-box creativity.

Character, substance, and inevitability are formed every time you are purposeful in your actions.

Power-25
Resolve-Power

Every day is different when you are living a constructive life and accomplishing the day's aim. Plan out and determine the focal point of your specified journey. Let the Resolve-Power always travel with you, setting your course of action to ensure your mode of resoluteness.

Improve yourself and watch your surroundings follow suit.

Power-26
Ameliorate-Power

Your external environment is grown and developed within the mindset, the mind is where you have the capability to influence and augment your life. When you improve yourself there, you will start to revisit your view, your contemplation upon your world, taking notice of the difference in your mental state. The time has come to understand how you might be casting your thoughts to the wind, with some thoughts populating and growing as a radiant sunflower, and others spreading the seeds of an annoying dandelion weed. I spend the time thinking about my thinking, a firm and fastened practice of mine. Empower yourself with the Ameliorate-Power, transforming life and its surroundings for your long-term sustainable betterment.

Work to slay doubt; it will kill your fear.

Power-27
Credence-Power

Recognize and embrace your intelligence, your gifts, and your talents; they are uniquely yours; there is no doubt. Never let your fears chase what you aspire and what you dream away. How you apply your distinctiveness is exclusive unto you, and you are here to find out what it is all about. Your Credence-Power must be secured by your willingness to know the expertise your experiences have given. Without welcoming this certainty about you, the things you hope for won't last for long, or more importantly, they won't come true. Admit and accept what you know how to do!

Don't waste your time, energy, or thought complaining about a complainer; doing so makes you a complainer, too.

Power-28
Endurance-Power

Your Endurance-Power will be in high demand while in the days of experiencing pronounced complaining. Look deep inside you to see if the initial complaining sparks off when you deliver your protest to your neighbor's door, setting the tone for how most everyone you connect with shall spend their precious day. If this might be your cause, then turn this outcome around by making sure to dispense your vitality on lifting others up with your words, including the words directed at you. In the case that someone does offer their complaining to you, consider that most likely their complaint did not begin with you, making their complaint not yours to own. You shall be known for being wise in the land for never turning around and sending the grumbles given into new ears, intervening in starting the process again and again.

People who tell you that you can only master one thing well don't know the power from whence they came.

Power-29
Self-Mastery-Power

The Self-Mastery-Power makes you the maker and the master of your own sway, your self-control. When one learns to be the supreme overlord of themselves with love, they gain the intuitiveness to master anything that they genuinely love. Behold and recognize the full worth of your supreme power. Once you have decided who you want to be, stay on track to triumph in that! Forever keep your self-mastery practice up to date.

Your mind is your most powerful tool; finetune it every day.

Power-30
Contemplation-Power

Keep the mind sharpened like precious cut stone; it is your diamond, your beautifully carved piece of art, and your most indispensable essential instrument. Work with its inventiveness in all moments of the waking day, taking nothing from its intellect and what it produces for granted. Regard it as your concealed treasure because that is what it is. Operationalize your mind and confer on its power to obtain the best performance, magnifying its intricate and delicate motif. Treat it like your first love, protecting it at all costs; this will be your lifelong task for having ongoing use of the Contemplation-Power.

Don't let your ego be in control even though it wants to be.

Power-31
Altruistic-Power

Too much self-importance can make you appear as pompous and vainglorious. Don't let this be your unintended objective. Stand out as being magnanimous, extending yourself with a selflessness force. Your Altruistic-Power will be like presenting a hummingbird to a nectar-filled flower.

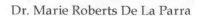
Make all conditions serve you.

Power-32
Intellectual-Power

Look for the benefits in all circumstances that enter your realm, and space. Dig beyond the fluff of what appears to be on the surface of any given place. Center yourself and prepare for building up your set of conditions; you can do it and let no one tell you any different. Find the concealed zone and examine what's in your territory for you to discover. Whether you perceive things to be good or bad, grasp what is there for you to learn and become competent about your environmental factors. Take your stance and grasp the reins of your Intellectual-Power.

Your world is populated with people who need your call to service and what you know to do. Be ready to support them.

Power-33
Magnanimity-Power

Are we not driven to show up for one another in our unique way? For those impacted, the positives that are done matter so much, whether the generosity is offered to the person next door or to the stranger and their family who we may never meet. At times we think twice about and ponder if our act of assistance makes a difference. I say to you, never hesitate to heed that inner call, for it is one step closer for all of life in blending our creative collective. Your piece in restoring our joint Magnanimity-Power.

Looking to the right or the left, you lose your way all your distractions will be open to bare. Your path might have twist and turns; watch for cliffs. The journey you seek is straight ahead; life balance.

Power-34
Certitude-Power

An unanticipated call just came in and took you off your focus. Let go of your culminating resistance to succeed at whatever is the enterprise. You must now take command to get yourself centered because what you do today will define your tomorrows. Submerge into your core of confidence because you have done the work to know who you are, as well as what you shall self-direct and perform. You are mentally muscular and choose to keep yourself on track. For you already know, you have been handpicked to fulfill your given path because the Certitude-Power has led you through to self-discovery of your way to *the Way*.

Know who you believe you are because if you don't, people will attempt to speak things into you based on who you unknowingly project yourself to be.

Power-35
Discernment-Power

Know who you let in your environment because their mirror image will reveal your Achilles heel about you, to you. Your reflection will not cast a lie no matter how hard you might try to deny. Use your given Discernment-Power in first pinpointing your perception of you.

*If what you consider as your power
is based on your money or your
position, then you really have none.*

Power-36
Potent-Power

Many carry the belief that if they obtain a better career and gather as much money and wealth as possible, they will have "power," not understanding power is not based on material wealth, assets, or a position. Believe this; your power is not based on the physical or the things external to you.

The power I speak of makes you victorious from within, the untouchable place where you thrive where you live. It cannot be taken away; it can only be given away if not held to be dear. You hold an enduring power from the light of your vibrancy; this power is persuasive, affecting, and is derived from having inner strength. It is vital to always keep this power lit, never letting it become diminished because it might if not cherished. Make it your business to spend time each day doing a daily power deposit; to the light, that is the mixology of you when you are functioning at your very best. With the use of your Potent-Power, you live out what you dream.

The mind does not agree with your decision to learn to multi-task, undermining its performance.

Power-37
Herculean-Power

How many tasks can be done at the same time, 100% well? Try it out, and you will see that it is not possible. Perform each of your task one at a time, never mixing them together, increasing your brain performance and potentiality. Taking on this quest of cerebrum utilization, you will experience, how much more dynamically efficient your accomplishments have become. Now, getting extraordinarily more things done? The Herculean-Power, when appropriately used, is sharpened to a tune in your mindset, supersizing and executing what you can do.

Working on a positive mindset requires effort every day. More effort than maintaining your healthy teeth. A common thread in both is if you don't take care as they delicately grow, they will rot and decay, becoming useless. Let go of the negative thoughts you previously preserved to ensure your psyche won't decompose.

Power-38
Exertion-Power

You must practice daily the self-work you do to get your mind clear, removing suffering in thought and emotion, so that you don't slip into dark spaces of mental despair. Be mindful of your Exertion-Power, as it influences your quality of thought.

An opportunity means nothing and never becomes real unless you do something with it.

Power-39
Connectedness-Power

There is no guarantee that your manifestations—your gifts that you have been given—will hang around forever, waiting for you to do something with them. Often, things don't circle back to the same door. So, if you give up on making use of your provided utensils, termed as your Personal-Power™, or even take them for granted, one day you might turn around to see they have walked on, enjoying life without you, beckoning to the call of someone who does not resemble you.

Your Connectedness-Power links you to your auspicious state. Note that you are not saying "no thank you" to what you fear about your potential opportunity; you are saying no thank you to your *Creator*, who, by the way, just opened the door you appealed to have unlocked.

When your intent is to teach someone a lesson, you end up being the one who gets taught.

Power-40
Principal-Power

People will surprisingly show up at any given moment of each day to speak words to you, over you, and about you, attempting to have supreme authority over your sensibility. If you don't have the foundational emotional posture and are grounded in knowing what you think, embrace, and believe about you, you will experience a turbulent mental state. Represent what you think and say about yourself, continually evolving your personal practice of your Principal-Power.

Learn the language of inner strength.

Power-41
Resolute-Power

Self-control, emotional firmness, and your ability to self-regulate are all a part of the stalwartness that represents your self-efficacy, decide to achieve. The Resolute-Power will never allow you to bathe yourself in defeat and watch your life go by as you flounder. After all, you are never failing; you are teaching yourself how you win.

Don't get the infectious disease that is verbally formed as gossip.

Power-42
Veracity-Power

Removing gossip and those who gossip from within your midst is vital for your well-being. Smiling on when within earshot of a gossiper's grin makes you a willing participant. By listening to the gossiper chatter, your mental capabilities are disrupted, wasting energy spinning in rumination. If by chance, you decide to share such gossip, you are helping to give it everlasting life and solidifying the contagion. Keep a lookout so the gossiper won't become a mainstay for what shows up to greet you at some point within each day throughout the rest of your life.

To get out of this troublesome situation, you must effectively use your shield known as your Veracity-Power.

Be known for the good you do in the world and not for what you have.

Power-43
Equanimity-Power

The higher intellect, also known as people, is here to do no harm; the higher intellect is here to do only good. Your *Creator* is waiting on you to discover that! So, with steady composure and profound self-poise, you will find the path of least resistance contained within you to do your good, filling up your joy. With your Equanimity-Power in full display, your emotional balance will lay the pathway for the healing of life.

Be the maker and the master of yourself.

Power-44
Radiance-Power

Are you living life, or is life living you as stress, depression, or anxiety? Have you been rushing through your daily existence with little memory of yesterday or even yesteryear? Life cannot be fulfilling if there is no time to "Be" with and for you in each moment. It is crucial for you to slow down and give to yourself even just 15 minutes to look, to view, and then clutch what is happening for you. For in the darkest of chambers, there is still light. Your counterglow is always there; it burns deep within, making you illuminated and brilliant founded in your Radiance-Power.

Nobody can beat you at "being" you.
Become extraordinarily best at it.

Power-45
Unparallel-Power

Be the expert in doing you, your prospects are high in perfecting that! You are an original created ideally in the daily image you see. So, why in the world would you want to be anybody other than you? Be enthralled in your unique and particular purpose and your passion. Understand that we are each trying to get to the same place on a different pathway; we are just doing different things to get us there while looking unalike. Remember, our personal journeys called life are uniquely prescribed for the individual.

Recognize the Unparallel-Power that makes you, you.

When you are unable to accept what you do, living life filled in denial, you are diminishing yourself and hindering your ability to embrace who and all that you are, and can accomplish.

Power-46
Empowerment-Power

You don't have to try to forget or pretend to forget your past harmful deeds; just don't live life there anymore. Today, you are given another chance to remedy what you didn't like in your days gone by. To make your world the one you seek to embrace that is held in your heart vision, drop the notion that you can't move on.

The Empowerment-Power, in its calmness and stillness, is waiting for you to take notice of your unquestionable resourcefulness to transform from all your life lessons that you now contain from within, which is the principal place where life makes the momentous difference.

Love is not transactional; love is unconditional. Give it out freely everywhere and to all of life you meet.

Power-47
Zeal-Power

Some believe that you must know someone to give them love. If that is true, how is it that a baby is born to instantaneous love? If you have given or experienced that type of love, you are able to see that giving love does not require you to know beforehand who you are giving it to or what you are giving it for. Ask of yourself to give to another an effortless try at this everyday solution; have the intent to look at as many "Beings" as you can directly in the eye and smile at them unconditionally with your heart, making a bodacious use of your Zeal-Power.

Be an extraordinary listener by listening for the positive and true intentions that will provide the key to unlock your mind and open any door.

Power-48
Harkening-Power

Because you think a thought from your listening of others, don't always give yourself permission to say it. Most times, people want to be heard and act out until someone pays attention, attempting to understand what they have to say. So, with compassion and care, grin and bear with what you are hearing. Consider that listening is the gift you will be giving that you might often wish to be given to you, your Harkening-Power.

Your patience will be your highest calling.

Reflect what your Creator does and not the shell of thyself. Be that!

Power-49
Cultivation-Power

How do you remedy your personal relationships? Outgrow them in understanding by removing your fixed mindset and reflecting onto them who you perceive them to be, never considering who they are or their life phenomenon. Identify and acknowledge for yourself that instead of doing you, you have decided to reflect and do your version of them. Doing so, you hand over your inner power: the control of your essence and the mirror of who you are.

So, today, choose to create the reflections that you want to translate from beyond your looking glass. Make a firm determination on how you want to keep fulfilling your life mission with the Cultivation-Power, thus expanding the field of your growth mindset.

Someone else or something may be able to divert your path, but you are the only one who can stop it. So, don't get distracted.

Power-50
Focal-Point-Power

People and things that we are not ready or willing to take on can get in front of us, mixing up our positive ideas and leading us astray from the path we thought we were set on. Stopping in those moments of distraction and doubt to close one's eyes and take a deep breath before moving on can prevent a great deal of calamity from heading your way.

Maintain your Focal-Point-Power, avoiding all thoughts that might divert you from your spiritual spotlight.

Affirm your stance and believe in your dreams; your future results will showcase your success.

My Daily Mantra

I come from my Creator; I have the same power as my Creator within me, and my power works with me to build the life I desire. I wield my Personal-Power™ *wisely as a creator just like my Creator.*

Acknowledgments

When I was in my search to locate the best within me and about me, there were individuals who showed up when I needed someone the most, no matter how ugly, mean, or wrong I was offering up their kindness.

To my loving lifelong friends, Gloria, Debra, Jacqueline, Etha, Kelly, Justin, and Barry thank you. My father, Tommy Roberts Jr., who is daily on my mind and left his physical existence when I was 22, instilled in me the drive to go after what I love. I miss and love you. To the Kimbrough's, I recognize I was one of your most significant challenges; I am grateful for your patience, and I love you both dearly! To B and Miss Mara, you each bring me extraordinary joy and fill up my heart. To my grandson, Pete (a blue Boston terrier), you taught me what love looks like when given unconditionally. You were an exceptional being and a great role model.

To all those who made even the tiniest of effort to support my goals, know that it is invaluable. You have my sincere appreciation.

I appreciate each of you and the power-filled life you live.

Love you much,
Marie

About the Author

Dr. Marie Roberts De La Parra is committed to global wellbeing and environmental causes, spending her career developing connectedness across various arenas and communities, including the non-profit sector, community and economic development, the small business pipeline, micro-finance, access to affordable business capital, academia for education awareness and empowerment, and government channels at a state, regional, federal, and international level.

Marie is the Chief Emotional Officer and founder at Wait a Green Minute, providing executive, business, and leadership coaching with the Life Energy Management System she designed. Inside this book, insight is shared into the foundational practice of the L.E.M. philosophy. Her strategy is to help her clients "introduce you to the more dynamic you" to maximize and showcase their inner strengths, illuminating the life essence for a positive state of extraordinariness.

Over the years, Marie has contributed to news articles, magazines, educational forums, and books focused on leadership. In 2019, she was one of the one hundred contributors to the Amazon bestseller in three categories, 1Habit™. Her 1Habit™ is number seven on the list. Her next book is underway.

Printed in the United States
by Baker & Taylor Publisher Services